EYE ON ART

# Fashion Design

## Clothing as Art

By Ruth Huoh

LUCENT PRESS

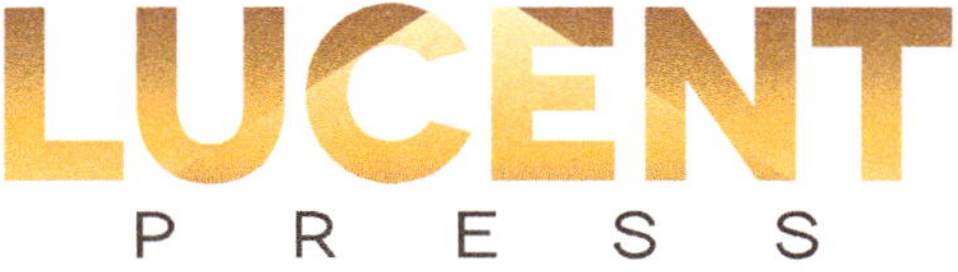

Published in 2018 by
**Lucent Press, an Imprint of Greenhaven Publishing, LLC**
353 3rd Avenue
Suite 255
New York, NY 10010



Designer: Seth Hughes
Editor: Vanessa Oswald

**Cataloging-in-Publication Data**

Names: Huoh, Ruth.
Title: Fashion design: clothing as art / Ruth Huoh.
Description: New York : Lucent Press, 2018. | Series: Eye on art | Includes index.
Identifiers: ISBN 9781534561045 (library bound) | ISBN 9781534561052 (ebook)
Subjects: LCSH: Fashion design–Juvenile literature. | Fashion–Juvenile literature.
Classification: LCC TT507.H86 2018 | DDC 746.9'2 –dc23

Printed in the United States of America

CPSIA compliance information: Batch #BS17KL: For further information contact Greenhaven Publishing LLC, New York, New York at 1-844-317-7404.

Please visit our website, www.greenhavenpublishing.com. For a free color catalog of all our high-quality books, call toll free 1-844-317-7404 or fax 1-844-317-7405.

# Contents

# Foreword

When many people think of art, the first things that come to mind may be paintings, drawings, sculptures, or even pictures created entirely with a computer. However, people have been applying artistic elements to almost every aspect of life for thousands of years. Human beings love beautiful things, and they seek beauty in unlikely places. Buildings, clothes, furniture, and many other things we use every day can all have an artistic aspect to them.

Attempts to define art have frequently fallen short. Merriam-Webster defines art as "something that is created with imagination and skill and that is beautiful or that expresses important ideas or feelings." However, almost no one refers to the dictionary definition when attempting to decide whether or not something can be considered art. They rely on their intuition, which leaves much room for debate between competing opinions. What one person views as beautiful, another may see as ugly. An idea that an artist feels it is important to express may hit home with some people and be dismissed by others. Some people believe that art should always be beautiful, while others feel that art should be unsettling enough to pull people out of their comfort zone. With all of these contradictory views, it is no wonder that the question of what is art is so often disputed.

This series aims to introduce readers to some of the more unconventional and controversial art forms, such as anime, fashion design, and graffiti. Debate on these topics has often been heated, with some people firmly declaring that they are art and others declaring just as firmly that they are not. Each book in the series discusses the history of a particular art form, the ways it is created, and the reasons why it is considered artistic. Learning more about these topics helps young adults recognize the art that is all around them as well as form their own opinions about this complex subject.

Quotes by experts in various art fields enhance the engaging text. All quotes are cited so readers can trace them back to their original source, giving them a starting point for further research. A list of recommended books and websites also allows young adults to delve deeper into related subjects. Full-color photographs give vivid examples of the artistic works being described in the books so readers can visualize the terms they are learning.

Through this series, young adults gain a better understanding of a variety of popular art forms. They also develop a deeper appreciation for the artistry that is inherent in the things they see and use every day.

INTRODUCTION

# The Evolution of Fashion

Fashion has been an integral part of society since prehistoric times. Cave paintings and remnants of clothing from that era have intricate beading, showing that even during a period of hunting and gathering, the time-consuming task of sewing beads into clothing was still considered important. No one has determined the exact reason why people began to wear clothes, but reasons vary from modesty, to protection from weather, to a way to display wealth.

Early humans wore pelts from animals they had killed. Cloth was not used as a clothing material until society began to settle down. People needed to plant cotton and herd sheep to get the materials for cloth. Cloth also required people to settle in a place long enough to create a structure to house a loom. The Industrial Revolution dramatically reduced the time needed to create clothing, and now the fashion industry moves at a tremendously fast pace, with new clothing entering some stores daily.

Fashion designs have often been puzzling to many. A person may wonder if there is truly any art to designing clothing, and this question is explored through the history of fashion design and different fashion techniques.

## Types of Fashion

There are three main categories of fashion design: haute couture, prêt-à-porter, and mass market. *Haute couture*,

This model is showing off the fashion design style known as haute couture, which must follow very specific rules.

which means "high sewing" in French, indicates handcrafted and custom-made creations made out of the highest quality fabrics. In 1945, the Chambre Syndicale de la Haute Couture in Paris created specific rules that a fashion label, or house, must follow to call itself a haute couture house. For a designer to be considered haute couture, it must meet all of these criteria and be invited by the Chambre Syndicale. These rules were updated in 1992:

- At least 35 pieces of day and evening wear must be presented twice a year during the spring and summer season in January, and during the autumn and winter season in August.

- These fashion designs must be custom-made for private clients, and include multiple model fittings. These designs can take anywhere from 100 to 1,000 hours to complete, and typically include luxury details such as St. Gallen lace and hand-sewn pearls.

- Finally, the designer must have a physical studio in Paris that employs a minimum of 15 full-time workers.

Haute couture pieces generally cost thousands of dollars to create and are exquisite works of art. However, the need for customized clothing has shrunk now, and haute couture has gradually been replaced in popularity with prêt-à-porter.

Ready-to-wear, or *prêt-à-porter* in French, refers to collections that are shown seasonally but use standardized sizes instead of customized fittings. These designs still use quality fabrics, construction, and close attention to detail, but they are more cost-effective to manufacture because they do not require customized fittings. Ready-to-wear collections now generate more profit than haute couture collections because of the time and cost associated with haute couture. Many haute couture designers also have prêt-à-porter lines.

Finally, mass-market designs began to explode in the late-19th century as a result of the Industrial Revolution. Manufacturing innovations during this time made it easier and faster to produce standardized clothing with little regard to quality or minute details. These designs are typically inspired from ready-to-wear collections. Mass-market retailers are able to create large quantities of standardized pieces and have reduced the production timeline to just a few weeks.

Understanding that there are three distinct types of fashion design can help young fashion designers pinpoint which category they want to work in.

Shown here is a model walking down the runway at a Marchesa show during New York Fashion Week. Marchesa is a fashion brand that produces both prêt-à-porter and haute couture clothing.

## Fashion Before Fashion Designers

The fashion industry has grown and changed over the millennia, and each year now brings in more than "$1.2 trillion, with more than $250 billion spent in the U.S. alone."[1] It affects everyone in society and has evolved from simple animal coverings to million-dollar, diamond-encrusted dresses that take months to complete. Toward the end of the 18th century, the industrial and commercial revolutions caused an increase in clothing production and manufacturing that created today's fashion industry. Clothing is now no longer designed just to keep you warm, but also as statements of art that utilize modern innovations in technology.

The first pieces of clothing were undoubtedly made out of animal skin and fur. Somehow, people discovered a way to soften the skins by rubbing oil into them. This made the pelts more comfortable to wear. It was now also possible to sew the furs together into bigger pieces, which they did with bone needles and thread.

As people began to settle in areas, production of cloth began. Civilizations such as the Egyptians and Greeks all draped large pieces of cloth over their bodies, with no cutting or sewing. Ironically, tailored clothing was considered barbaric, while simple, draped clothing was the mark of civilization. The Roman Empire, which ruled Europe for hundreds of years, has influenced much of Europe's clothing designs.

One of the most well-known pieces of clothing is the Roman toga. Draping this large piece of cloth required both art and skill.

## Marie Antoinette

In 1770, Marie Antoinette of Austria made the journey to France to marry Louis XVI, who became that nation's king. As the new queen of France, with little to amuse herself with, she became addicted to shopping. She spent extravagant amounts of money, buying precious jewels and ordering hundreds of dresses and shoes for herself each year. Women of the French court all tried to replicate her style, especially at the wild masquerade parties that the queen held. Sheltered with her husband in the palace known as Versailles, Antoinette ignored angry criticism from the French public. She continued to spend extravagant amounts of money on clothing, while France's citizens starved in the streets, which ultimately led to the downfall of the French monarchy. Antoinette's style still influences many fashion designers today.

Togas were mainly a garment for the upper class because they prevented free movement. Senators only wore togas in white. As the Roman Empire expanded, Eastern cultures began to influence designs, especially after the Western Roman Empire fell in AD 476. Constantinople was then cut off from the Western world, and clothing in this part of the world became colorful, embellished with embroidery, tassels, fringe, and jewels. Although it was a long and costly journey to get the fabric, silk from China also became popular.

During the Crusades from 1095 to 1291, the Muslim world's influence made an appearance in fashion trends, with some European women adopting veils to cover their faces. Francesca Sterlacci and Joanne Arbuckle wrote, "Most historians agree that the origin of fashion trends started in the Middle Ages, a time when social and economic changes created a demand for fashionable goods."[2] During the Renaissance, which originated in Italy, Italian fashion dominated, and fashion trends began to move from country to country via marriages and travels. The royal families were seen as fashion role models, most notably Queen Isabella of Spain and Catherine de' Medici of France.

With nationalism on the rise during the 1600s, rulers attempted to stop their citizens from wearing clothes from other countries, but they were all fairly unsuccessful. At the same time, these same rulers of England, France, and Italy were all fighting for control of the fashion scene. Spain had prevailed in 1492, after Christopher Columbus successfully landed in the Americas, but no one country had ever established its dominance permanently. The Enlightenment period of the 1700s encouraged tremendous growth in the arts, especially in regards to textile and fashion development. Other improvements during the Enlightenment also helped to pave the way for the Industrial Revolution.

In France, beginning with the support of King Louis XIV, French fashion and textiles were heavily promoted. This support continued through his heirs Louis XV and Louis XVI and his wife, Marie Antoinette. The queen even had her own personal fashion designer, Rose Bertin, who she called "the Minister of Fashion." The dominant style during Louis XIV's reign was baroque—full of rich, dark fabrics and elaborate designs. It quickly became known throughout Europe that French textiles and materials were of the highest quality. Louis XIV successfully made his Court of Versailles the fashion authority that influenced all of Europe, setting the path for France's future reign as the fashion capital of the world.

The Industrial Revolution, which began in the late 1700s, revolutionized the fashion industry with inventions such as the cotton gin and the spinning jenny. These two products significantly reduced the time that it took to produce cotton and cloth. Instead of making clothes by hand, clothes were now being made by machines. Mass production of clothing began.

The French Revolution in 1789 had a huge impact on French fashion. The previously popular embroidered coats and gowns were all abandoned. Women threw away bustles, corsets, and rich textiles, choosing simple muslin and calico garments instead, which was a huge shift from the extravagance of Marie Antoinette's era. As Napoleon Bonaparte's reign in France began in the early 1800s, many continued to look to the royal family as fashion icons. Unlike Marie Antoinette, the Empress Josephine mainly followed the trends that the dressmakers were setting. However, she was still influential through her preference of empire waist dresses and Kashmir shawls. This influence was again seen throughout Europe.

Queen Victoria ascended to the British throne in 1837, and thus began the Victorian Era. Due to her height of 5 feet (152 cm), the fashion during this time consisted of a tight chest, natural waist, and bell-shaped skirt. This style flattered the petite queen. She primarily wore British-made clothing, and she strongly encouraged her court to do so as well. During this era, corsets were a required part of women's fashion. Crinolines and hoop

*Marie Antoinette, who was the queen of France around the time of the French Revolution in the late 1700s, was known for wearing extravagant attire.*

skirts, both of which were worn to create the sense of voluminous skirts, were also popular.

France continued its own fashion dominance with Empress Eugénie, wife of Napoleon III. It was around the time of her reign that the fashion design industry began in earnest. The Industrial Revolution's inventions worked to bring about the emergence of fashion as an industry. The increased demand for clothing also prompted the industry to create standardized sizes for easier production. All of these factors helped to create the profitable fashion design industry.

# CHAPTER ONE

# History of Fashion Design

Fashion design traces its roots back to Paris in the 1850s, with the rise of haute couture. Since then, fashion trends and designs have evolved, changing every few years based on economic and global events, such as World War I or the rise of the Internet. As globalization increased, Paris lost its position as the sole fashion capital of the world, and now people are following their own trends, influenced by different cultures and styles around the world.

## Rise of Fashion Before World War I

Paris had established itself as the global capital of fashion during the reign of King Louis XIV. In 1858, Englishman Charles Frederick Worth, an émigré to France, opened the first known haute couture fashion house in Paris. His designs were so loved there that he became the first person to start dictating his trends to his wealthy clients, instead of them telling him what they wanted. His clients included Empress Eugénie, Empress Elisabeth of Austria, actresses Sarah Bernhardt and Lillie Langtry, and opera singer Jenny Lind. He is widely known as the father of haute couture. Other designers soon followed suit by opening their own haute couture houses in Paris.

Fashion trends began to debut at horse races, and *Vogue* and other fashion magazines became popular by reporting what designs were in style to the rest of the world. Fashion magazines are still important today,

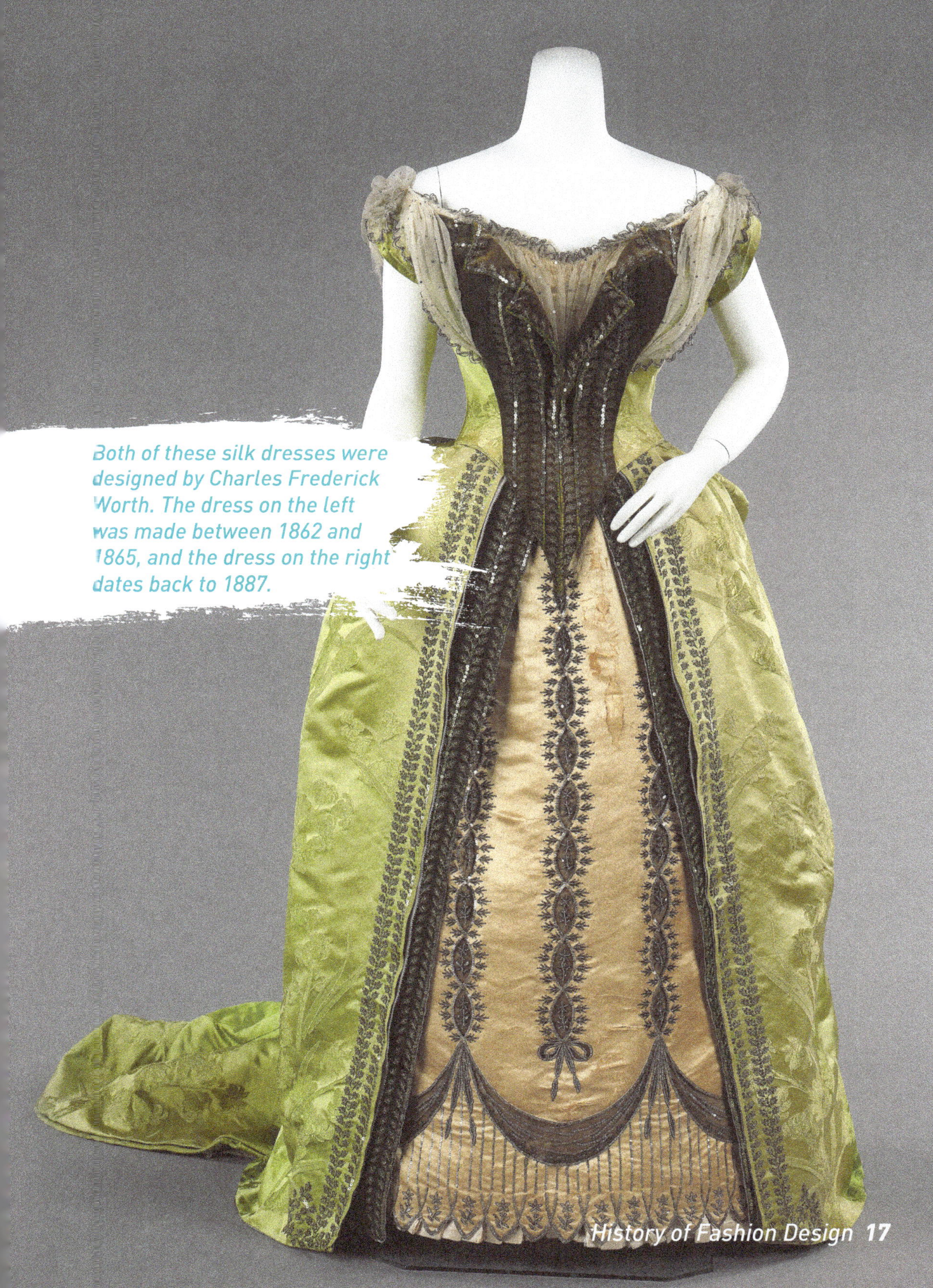

Both of these silk dresses were designed by Charles Frederick Worth. The dress on the left was made between 1862 and 1865, and the dress on the right dates back to 1887.

Corsets were used to create fashionable curvy silhouettes with tiny waists, despite how uncomfortable it was to wear one. Women also wore gigantic hoop skirts and large bustles to complement the outfit proportionally. Dressing against fashion trends at this time resulted in social ridicule and gossip. Everyone chose what they wore according to social status: The privileged wore new clothes that included yards and yards of fabric, and servants were restricted to wearing second-hand clothes, mainly in black. As the Art Nouveau movement grew in popularity, the neutral and pastel colors that were previously favored gave way to more vibrant colors with the invention of synthetic dyes.

Frenchman Paul Poiret rose into prominence during the early 1900s and broke the silhouette from the curvy figure that required a corset to a leaner line. He was completely devoted to design. He has been praised for his "dedication to the art of dress" and has been called "a master of colour, texture and fabrics."[3] His designs were loosely draped on women and did not require the hoops and skirts that women were used to wearing. Harem pants that he designed were so groundbreaking that they caused riots and arrests when women wore them in public. However, Poiret then took a step back when he created the infamous hobble skirt in 1910, a narrow skirt that restricted women from taking large strides, forcing them to hobble around. Despite his influence in the world of fashion, Poiret's extravagant lifestyle led him to die a homeless and penniless man.

## The Little Black Dress (LBD)

In 1926, Coco Chanel debuted the "little black dress" (LBD), which was featured in *Vogue*. Before her influence, black was mainly worn by servants on a daily basis or by someone in mourning. Because of the massive amount of deaths in World War I, black was being worn more often in society. Chanel's LBD created the idea that black could be worn in an elegant and flattering way all the time, not just during mourning. Rhonda Garelick wrote, "Chanel turned the color of mourning into a global trend."[1]

*Vogue* correctly predicted that the design of the dress was similar in nature to the Ford Model T design, calling it "The Chanel 'Ford'—the frock that all the world will wear."[2] It was easily mass-produced and widely adopted by the market, and like the Ford vehicle, it was accessible to women of all social levels. Black is now no longer associated with just servants or mourning but has become a chic color, perfect for any outfit.

1. Rhonda K. Garelick, *Mademoiselle Coco Chanel and the Pulse of History*. New York, NY: Random House, 2014, p.198.
2. Garelick, *Mademoiselle Coco Chanel*, p. 199.

*This photograph of a model wearing a Chanel little black dress appeared in a 1926 issue of Vogue. This kind of dress is still very popular today. Fashion runways and clothing stores around the world are filled with LBDs.*

Then, with the start of World War I, fashion took a dramatic change, especially as women shifted in society to fill in for the work of men who were away at war. Short hair and an androgynous silhouette became popular, moving away from the previous extravagant fashions in solidarity with the war. Military elements, such as roomy pockets and trench coats, were woven into designs, and khaki became the new "it" color.

Coco Chanel was one of the most influential women in fashion during this time, and she still is today. She was famous not only for her quotes, such as "A girl should be two things: classy and fabulous,"[4] but also for her successful innovations. Because of World War I's fabric rationing, designers had to experiment with different materials for clothing. One important innovation Chanel had was to use jersey material for everyday clothes. This material had traditionally only been used for men's underwear. Now, women were able to wear clothing made out of a material that was comfortable and easy to move around in. This made it easier for them to perform the jobs that men had traditionally held. Chanel showed her first collection in 1913, and she created simple, wearable, yet elegant designs. Her clothing helped to remove the corset from women's fashion again. She also made it trendy for women to wear many items from men's apparel, including blazers, shirts, and trousers. Because of her influence, trousers were no longer seen as just utilitarian or eccentric to wear. Her brand is still successful today and follows the same philosophy of creating simple yet elegant products.

## The Great Depression and World War II

After World War I, the 1920s brought about a change where women either returned to the traditionally feminine dress or adopted the modern. The romantic style involved flowing dresses in gauzy organza and taffeta. The dresses were adorned with ribbons, lace, and flowers in pastel colors. In direct opposition to this look was the *garçonne* look, which spoke to women's desire for social freedom. This style included short hair and straight-cut dresses with dropped waists at hip-level.

The Great Depression that began in 1929 helped to bring fashion of all classes to a similar look. In general, there was a return to a more feminine look with soft, flowing dresses. All industries were hit during the Depression, especially fashion. European designers could no longer depend on sales from the Americans, and this hindered couturiers the most, since their designs cost the most. Many designers had to close their stores, while others began to diversify into ready-to-wear lines.

Main Bocher was the first American fashion designer to open a haute couture house in Paris. He changed his name to Mainbocher when he established himself as a premier designer. What was exceptional about him was that he managed to do this in the middle of the Great Depression, a time when everyone else around him was struggling just to survive. Mainbocher was first a fashion illustrator for *Harper's Bazaar*, then the editor of French *Vogue*, before he made the decision to become a haute couture designer in his early 40s. He was commissioned to design the Duchess of Windsor's wedding dress in 1937, a public media event that catapulted him into overnight success. His designs were made almost entirely by hand, were simple and flattering, and were of the highest quality fabrics. He never created ready-to-wear designs, focusing only on haute couture with high prices. During World War II, instead of closing his fashion line like many of his counterparts, Mainbocher returned to the United States and held his first American show in 1940, which opened to a full house. Mainbocher enjoyed a successful 40-year career until he retired in 1971.

During and after the Great Depression, many people were searching for a way to escape their worries, so they flocked to the movies. Hollywood had a large influence on fashion during this time. Women's fashion silhouettes changed from a linear look to a softer, more feminine one, and hemlines were dropped. Women wanted to emulate their favorite glamorous Hollywood stars, such as Greta Garbo, Marlene Dietrich, or Joan Crawford. Fashion trends were created not only what was seen in films, but also what was worn by

Actress Greta Garbo, shown here, was one of many Hollywood stars women of the 1930s looked to for fashion inspiration.

stars offscreen. Backless evening gowns were created and became wildly popular, and furs were used extensively as accessories. During this time, Samuel Goldwyn, a successful Hollywood producer, formed a collaboration with Chanel for her to design costumes for his movie stars. Hollywood stars appreciated Chanel's elegant and simple designs offscreen, and Garbo and Dietrich were both her personal clients. However, Chanel's designs did not translate well into Hollywood's extravagant movies, so after spending a year there, she returned to France and went into retirement.

As fashion and art began to merge, Elsa Schiaparelli brought the surrealism movement into fashion design. Although untrained formally, "Schiap" was known for her innovative and shocking creations, especially her trompe-l'oeil sweaters and an elegant gown that featured a lobster painted by Salvador Dalí. She was the first to use wrap dresses, shoulder pads, animal prints, trompe l'oeil prints, and dyed-to-match zippers, and she was the first designer to issue press releases about her upcoming collections. Her shows were also extravagant affairs that included music, light shows, and acrobatic dances. She lived life by following her own advice: "Dare to be different."[5] Her ideas and

*Elsa Schiaparelli's shocking dresses included the one shown here, which had a lobster painted on it by Salvador Dalí.*

*Elsa Schiaparelli is shown here fitting a model with a dress in her shop in Paris while a worker checks the measurements.*

designs greatly influenced both her contemporaries and current fashion designers.

With the start of World War II, fabric rationing began to impact much of the Western world, with most of the fashion industry coming to a halt as the Nazis invaded France. Many designers were forced to shut their doors and flee to America, and as a result, Paris lost its place as the epicenter of fashion. London and New York City began to emerge as new fashion capitals, especially with the influx of designers to those locations. American designers began to focus more on creating their own fashion identity that reflected a more casual lifestyle. Domestic designers had to become trendsetters while struggling with the fabric rationing of the war. In the United States, Mainbocher, Norman Norell, and Claire McCardell were successful domestic fashion designers at this time.

Rayon, a substitute for silk, became popular after World War I, and it helped with the fabric rationing since silk was being used for manufacturing parachutes and gunpowder bags. As a result of women performing labor-intensive work that was generally reserved for men, pants and heavy-duty clothing became popular. Sportswear became

## Queen of the Bias Cut

Although largely unknown today, Madeleine Vionnet was a master designer and had an exquisite skill for cutting and draping. She was greatly influenced by the Cubism movement and its abstract representations of geometric shapes, along with ancient Greek and Roman dress. Vionnet's designs are recognizable due to her famous bias cut and other twists and pleats. The bias cut is a style of cutting fabric in which the fabric is not cut in parallel lines, but rather at 45-degree angles. This style of cutting created clothing that fluidly flowed around one's body in a flattering manner. Women loved Vionnet's designs.

Shown here is one of Madeleine Vionnet's dress designs from 1938 in a full view (right) and in a close-up image of its bodice (left).

Shown here is an evening dress made by Christian Dior, who created the "New Look" after World War II.

more popular as well, especially in the United States, which has since dominated in that domain.

After the end of World War II, many Paris designers returned to France, and eventually it became the fashion capital again. In 1947, Christian Dior exploded onto the Paris fashion scene with his visionary "New Look." A breath of fresh air after World War II, his collection consisted of rounded shoulders; slim, corseted waistlines; and calf-length skirts that consumed up to 25 yards (23 m) of fabric. It was in direct contrast to the fabric rationing of World War II and answered the longing for feminine clothes that woman had instead of the military look. Dior continued to innovate, creating brand new silhouettes with every new collection he produced. All of his collections reminded women of an elegant and romantic style and symbolized hope for a better future after the war. Dior is credited with putting Paris back on the map as the capital of fashion, although its influence was no longer as strong as it had been in the past.

## Post–World War II

In the 1950s, a mature, elegant fashion style emerged. Women wore tailored suits and shirtwaist dresses during the day and changed into fancy cocktail dresses and gowns in the evening. Hollywood idols once again became style icons, especially stars such as Marilyn Monroe, Elizabeth Taylor, Grace Kelly, and Audrey Hepburn. Since these film stars all wore different styles and looks, women could choose to dress in Doris Day's "girl-next-door" style or like Elizabeth Taylor in a more elegant style. During this time, Dior and his successor, Yves Saint Laurent, began to feature waist-less garments, which critics nicknamed "the sack."

Horrified by the way that these new male designers were creating unflattering clothes for women, at 70 years of age, Chanel came out of retirement in 1954. Her designs were always created with women in mind, looking for ways to liberate them through classic tweed suits, quilted bags with long golden chains to allow for free hands, and her famous little black dress (LBD). She refused to let women become confined in clothing designed by men, such as long, heavy skirts and stiff, tight jackets, when she had spent so much time and effort creating clothing that was comfortable and allowed women the freedom to move and do more than just stay at home.

Italian designers finally broke back into the fashion scene in the 1950s as well with bright colors and bold patterns. This style had a bright, youthful feel, and was popular with Americans. Emilio Pucci and Roberto Capucci were two of the most well-known Italian designers during this time. Pucci mainly designed casual clothes and sportswear in his famous colorful silk geometric prints. Capucci created collections that were inspired

by architecture and geometry and is best known for his boxy silhouette look, which was often complemented with large, square buttons.

"Baby boomers" are the children who were born after the end of World War II, when there was a huge increase in the birth rate. As the baby boomer population turned into teenagers and their disposable income increased, they began to have a heavy influence on fashion. From 1960 to 1967, teenagers were the focus of fashion designers. Designers began to market to the average young person, instead of just to the elite and wealthy. At first, Hollywood stars such as James Dean and Marlon Brando were influences, popularizing moto jackets and making the T-shirt a fashionable piece of clothing. Then, as Hollywood began to lose its influence among the younger generations, pop music stars, athletes, and fashion models rose to become the new fashion icons. Mick Jagger and David Bowie were two iconic music stars who influenced fashion trends. Fashion and music were then linked for the foreseeable future.

London became the new epicenter of fashion, especially in terms of catering to the teenage and youth culture. This crowd

Mary Quant, shown here, designed the iconic miniskirt, which was a must-have fashion item in the 1960s.

was characterized by being adventurous and willing to show it by wearing crazy outfits. The miniskirt, created by British designer Mary Quant, was the fashion item of the decade. Quant was a prolific designer, creating more than 28 collections, all of which were fun and wearable, created mainly for her teenage customers.

The 1960s also created a culture of throwaway clothes and resulted in many short-lived fashion fads. The throwaway fad grew to the extent where clothes were made out of paper and thrown away by many after one wear. Fads changed from year to year—from the iconic miniskirt, popularized by fashion model Twiggy, to brightly colored stockings and long, flared overcoats with military elements. Ready-to-wear clothing dominated the industry, instead of the haute couture pieces that most designers were used to creating. The "Space Race" between the United States and the Soviet Union, which was quickly taking over news, also inspired fashion designs, with collections of whites and metallics mixed with reinvented astronaut looks.

During this time, Oscar de la Renta came onto the fashion scene. He was the first American to create and show haute couture for a Paris house. His design elements mainly consisted of ruffles, precise tailoring, and quality workmanship. He wanted to create beautiful clothes for all women. Although he is known for his haute couture clothes, de la Renta also understood how important ready-to-wear lines were for business.

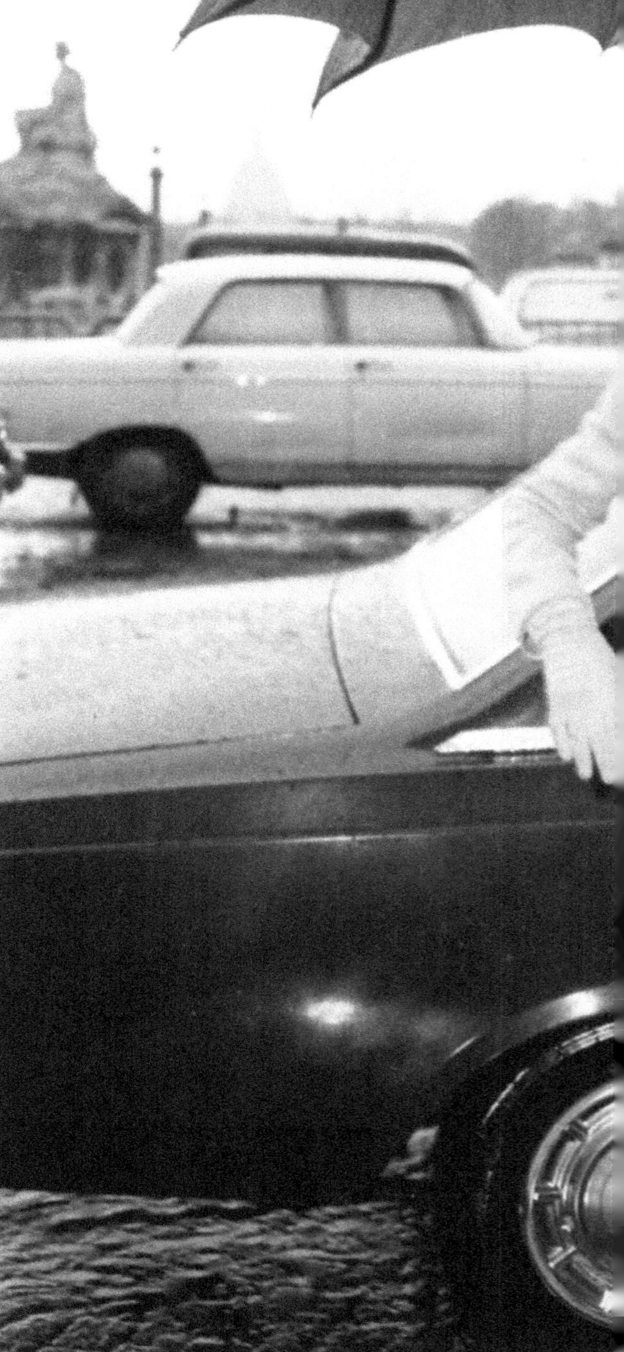

During the 1960s, Jacqueline Kennedy Onassis, commonly known

Jacqueline Kennedy Onassis, shown here, served as a fashion icon in the 1960s both during and after her time in the White House.

as Jackie, became a fashion icon who inspired millions as the First Lady of the United States and even after the death of her husband, President John F. Kennedy. Oleg Cassini, a family friend, was her personal couturier and designed more than 300 outfits for her, including her iconic pillbox hats. As the First Lady, she made many public appearances, and she was known for her chic and effortless style, especially her signature oversize sunglasses and headscarves. Her clean silhouettes and A-line dresses took over fashion, and her style still inspires many today.

As the Vietnam War began and then became increasingly unpopular and unemployment and inflation rates rose, the hippie movement began. This period was important as people began to question what they wore, and individuality eventually became dominant. Clothing during this time took a turn at looking handmade. Tie-dyed T-shirts and shirts with embroidered or hand-lettered sayings were popular. This was also when a more ethnic look became

Ralph Lauren, whose clothing is shown here, became a famous American designer in the 1970s.

popular, with items such as beaded knits and afghans attempting to show that people were rejecting the Western consumerist culture.

By the late 1970s, fashion had come full circle, where designers were no longer dictating trends to society, but individuals were choosing their own styles. The miniskirt is thought to be the last trend that was universally followed. A number of master fashion designers began to retire as ready-to-wear clothes began to become more popular and the haute couture industry declined. There was also a return to tailored, masculine designs, especially those of Ralph Lauren and Calvin Klein.

Paris had long been the capital of fashion. Even though many fashion designers had fled to the United States during World War II, their style was still European. When Ralph Lauren came along in the 1970s, he successfully capitalized on the American style. He disregarded the use of polyester and the hippie style, both of which were popular during this time, and focused instead on what he saw as decidedly American. He used multiple signature American styles, such as the iconic Ivy League prep style and the Western look with denim shirts and cowboy boots. His logo of a polo horse is now recognized globally. Lauren has since diversified his fashion house into other products and become one of the most successful American fashion designers.

Calvin Klein entered the fashion scene with his controversial advertising in the early 1970s. His scandalous marketing campaign, with Brooke Shields coyly asking, "You wanna know what comes between me and my Calvins? Nothing,"[6] sold hundreds of thousands of Calvin Klein (CK) jeans. Klein continued to capitalize on this personal formula of success, realizing that provocative advertising is just as important as the actual clothing. He also used clean lines to create tailored suits for women. In addition, Klein branded his logo proudly on the outside of the jeans pocket. He was the initiator of the logo mania that grew in popularity, peaking in the 1990s.

The 1970s also saw the emergence of Japanese designers into the Western fashion world. They breathed new life and style into traditional designs. Designers such as Kenzo Takada and Issey Miyake focused on loose, layered garments. Kenzo is known for being the first to stylistically blend elements from different countries together. Miyake's designs do not follow a body's silhouette, but instead break it up. He has grand visions of how a person can interact with their clothes geometrically. He also frequently uses the technique of pleating, which is a Japanese tradition. His pleated clothes are created with an innovative process that allows them to retain the pleats, even if the clothing becomes rumpled.

In 1976, the punk movement became popular in London, driven by unemployed youngsters who were aiming to shock. The look was typically

*Designer Calvin Klein started putting his logo on the outside of all the jeans he designed in the 1970s and continues to do so today.*

composed of black leather jackets and tight black pants with Doc Martens shoes. T-shirts with obscene images or words often accompanied the look. Vivienne Westwood and Malcolm McLaren were stylistic leaders of this movement, and McLaren's subsequent formation of the music group The Sex Pistols continued to spread the punk movement. Authors Valerie Mendes and Amy de la Haye wrote, "Ultimately, Punk had an energizing effect on British fashion and helped re-establish London's reputation for innovative youth style."[7] Although punk fashion started in London, it moved and spread to the United States and other countries as well. Punk also advanced from being a movement just amongst teens, who bought their clothes from secondhand stores, to being commercialized in mass markets and finally filtered into high fashion. This progression is typically the opposite in the fashion industry, so that makes this movement even more interesting. Punk still influences many designers today.

## Increased Marketing and Technology

Fashion in the 1980s shifted towards a more commercial look, showing how society was becoming more interested in money and image. Everything was big, including hair, jewelry, belts, and shoulder pads.

Branding has been an integral part of fashion ever since Louis Vuitton monogrammed his luggage in the early 1900s. Other famous logos include Chanel's intertwined Cs, and Prada's triangular metal logo. With society's shift to be image-conscious, marketing and branding exploded and became even more integral parts of fashion design. Designers used a variety of tactics to attempt to stand out as technology made it easier for consumers to choose clothes from any designer. Louis Vuitton's bags with the famous LV logo were seen everywhere, and Moschino's large belt buckles, Montblanc pens, and Rolex watches became "it" items.

The British royal family welcomed Princess Diana in the 1980s, and she immediately became a fashion icon worldwide. Princess Diana had a chic style that appealed to the mass markets. Regardless of whether she was attending public influential events or touring with the royal family, the outfits that she commissioned became popular. She was the figurehead for British fashion, and women all over the world followed her widely photographed outfits.

In 1982, Halston was the first fashion designer who collaborated with a mass-market retailer, JCPenney. It was an ill-fated partnership that made Halston into a laughingstock. At that point in time, high-end stores shunned Halston's move because they did not want such a close association with the common masses. Many stores dropped his lines, and the JCPenney line was unsuccessful commercially as well. Now, customers are fighting to get their hands on limited items from designer collaborations with stores such as Target, Wal-Mart, and H&M. Target's collaboration with Missoni sold out in minutes, both online and in stores.

After Chanel's death in 1971, her brand declined in popularity, with no clear vision, until Karl Lagerfeld was asked to take over in 1983. Many people doubted Lagerfeld's ability to revive the deteriorating label. Lagerfeld proved them all wrong when he reinvented Chanel's classic style in a contemporary manner that appealed to the younger market, while still retaining Chanel's original customers. He uses different signature elements of Chanel, such as pearls, tweed, or the "double C," in his collections. In addition, Lagerfeld has personally designed and photographed all of Chanel's ad campaigns. His perfectionist approach has been successful for the brand.

In the 1990s, more styles than ever appeared. There was no "one look" that everyone flocked to. Even fashion magazines had to change to convey the variety of styles on trend, instead of just focusing on one for the season. This was partly due to the fact that designers from Belgium, Austria, Sweden, African nations, and other countries were making their way into annual fashion shows with their unique designs. People could choose to follow influences from any

## What About Men?

Men's fashion has also seen dramatic changes since the 19th century, although it has not undergone as many changes as women's fashion. Instead of Paris, London, particularly Savile Row, has led men in fashion trends because the designers there are accepted as having superior tailoring skills. Extensive wardrobes were immaculately kept by servants for the men to be ready for any occasion. During the early 1900s, men were expected to carry a slender walking stick or umbrella.

In the 1930s, Hollywood greatly influenced men's style, with Cary Grant and Gary Cooper acting as icons for sleek tailoring. During World War II, as most men were in the military, dress became more casual, and the suit declined in popularity. In the 1980s, more designers began to embrace menswear lines as a viable market, including them in their shows each season. In the 1990s, Raf Simons created a slimmer, tailored silhouette, in opposition to the previous muscular silhouette. Other designers, such as Alber Elbaz and Tom Ford, have since followed suit.

Designer Tom Ford, shown here, has become one of the leaders in men's fashion in the 21st century.

Designer Angela Missoni launched her design collaboration, Missoni for Target, in 2014. This line was popular with consumers.

or all of these different designers. The "Modern Bohemian" look was the most prevalent of these, composed of mixing and layering different pieces, such as wearing dresses over pants or two different prints in the same outfit. Other designers found inspiration from the styles of the 1960s and 1970s.

During the late 1990s, utility clothing became popular, bringing a return to army chic. Designer Helmut Lang took previously unfashionable clothing, such as army surplus or parkas, and recreated them with rich textiles. The Gap also became popular for its hoodie and cargo pants, which became essentials for many wardrobes.

Runway collections began to show evidence of being influenced by street fashion, instead of the other way around. In addition, ready-to-wear collections became more dominant, with other cheaper, diffusion lines being featured on the runways as well. These in-between collections are popular with customers since they hit an affordable price point while still giving consumers products with the luxury brand name. The Internet and technology have continued to revolutionize not only the way fashion is designed, but also how people shop and decide what clothes they purchase. Ready-to-wear collections and mass retail clothing are now freely available for many people, not just the wealthy.

# Fashion Is Art

Fashion design has long been seen as a form of art and can be highly subjective. It can be influenced by any variety of things, including a designer's travels, background, roots, or even innate sense for design. One of the most important design principles for aspiring fashion designers is individual creativity. Successful fashion designers are always challenging themselves, reinventing past trends or finding inspiration in different places. Keeping an open mind—whether a person is wandering the markets of Morocco, exploring the Forbidden Palace in Beijing, or hanging out at their favorite pizza joint— allows designers to see that there are elements everywhere that can inspire them. Understanding current social, economic, and political trends also helps designers create relevant and successful fashion designs.

## What Can Influence Fashion Design?

The abundance of material on fashion trends throughout history makes the past a popular influence for designers. The fashion life cycle continually brings back trends that were popular in the past. There are a variety of silhouettes, details, fabrics, and colors throughout the centuries that designers use to influence their current work. Creative designer minds also enjoy taking past trends in fashion and reinterpreting them. Certain styles are often reinterpreted every few years by different designers. Corsets have gone in and out of style ever since the beginning of fashion design in the 1800s. Elements such as animal prints are typically included in a collection every season. A designer may find they are influenced by how hats were worn in the early 1800s or how dresses were draped in the 1950s. When using historical trends, designers consider how to update and adapt the historical designs to the needs of the contemporary market and not just how to produce the same trend again.

Architecture is another popular influence on fashion designs. It is another form of art that requires creativity, but it tends to be more structured than fashion design. Fashion designers can find inspiration based on the lines, curves, colors, textures, and points of view of a building. Many designers have favorite buildings or architects that inspire their collections. Fashion designer Phillip Lim's favorite building is the suburban home of architect Luis Barragán in Mexico City. This building is a precise balance of light, color, and shadow, which ties well into Lim's aesthetic of asymmetric silhouettes and bold colors. Another designer who draws from architecture is Milly's founder and designer, Michelle Smith. For her spring and summer 2016 collection, Smith drew from the works of the late architect Zaha Hadid. The designs balanced an oversized sculptural look with organic softness, similar to many of Hadid's designs.

The rich and diverse traditions of other cultures can also serve as inspiration for a collection. There are many important symbols and motifs of different cultures that can be reinterpreted in design. The rich and bold colors of Indian saris, the hamsa symbol of the Middle East, and Chinese characters such as love and peace have all been featured in many different fashion collections. When using these ethnic elements in designs, it is crucial for designers to remember the symbolism that is associated with each of them. Designers have to be careful not to be offensive with their designs, unless they are making a specific statement.

Motifs or symbols that are repeated throughout a collection to tie all the pieces together are also important design influences. A motif can be a particular shape, concept, or fabric. The motif is generally interpreted in several different ways so that the collection is cohesive but not repetitive and boring. Motifs can be of different colors, sizes, fabrics, and textures. Coming up with innovative ways to display the motif is all part of being a successful designer.

Technology is yet another influence impacting the way designers create their clothes. Its influence has increased as more innovative fabrics and methods to design are developed. There are smart textiles that wick away sweat, are UV-proof, and even change colors based on exposure to the sun. Wearable and smart technology are also becoming more popular.

*Shown here is the Heydar Aliyev Center Museum in Baku, Azerbaijan. The design for this structure was created by the late Zaha Hadid, whose unique architectural designs have influenced many fashion designers.*

*Actress Audrey Hepburn played the role of Holly Golightly in the1961 film* Breakfast at Tiffany's. *The LBD she wore inspired several fashion designs.*

Designers have begun to create collections based off of futuristic ideas, including how technology and humanity can become more integrated. There is a constant struggle between aesthetic and functionality in these designs. As technology continues to grow, more designers will start to integrate technology into their designs.

Another important design influence comes from films. Hollywood has influenced fashion design numerous times throughout the decades. Not only can a film influence design when it is first released, it can also inspire designers who watch it in the future. Audrey Hepburn's character in *Breakfast at Tiffany's* is a classic example of influencing fashion when it first debuted and continuing to influence women and LBD designs to this day. *Sex & the City* is another popular example, with Sarah Jessica Parker causing many women to fall in love with designer clothes and to dream of their own walk-in closets full of Manolo Blahnik shoes.

Proportions, such as if the designs are top heavy or bottom heavy, are another important consideration to a collection. Designers often exaggerate proportions for haute couture collections, and then the proportions tend to balance out in ready-to-wear collections. It is important for designers to keep proportions consistent on models for each collection. Practicing sketches helps to create the same type of body for each of their designs. There is also a 2:3 "golden ratio" that many designers follow, which creates the right balance and proportion to visually appeal to customers.

Another critical influence is color. Color is probably the most visual and striking of the design elements. Different colors evoke different emotions, and designers need to understand these emotions and how to use them successfully in their collections. They consider what emotions they want someone to feel when looking at their fashion collection. Additionally, they consider emotions they do not want the audience to feel. Some designers tend to stick to black and white palettes, such as Yohji Yamamoto and Rei Kawakubo. Other designers, such as Lilly Pulitzer and Emilio Pucci, use bright colors. Each of their collections is successful, but they speak to different audiences.

Texture and form compose the basic structure of any collection. A successful collection typically uses several different types of complementary fabrics of different weights. Using a complementary mixture of solids, patterns, and prints can also help to create a cohesive collection without boring the audience. However, while texture and silhouettes are important elements, emphasizing both will overpower and confuse the audience. A successful designer will allow the fabric to naturally flow over the wearer.

# Evolution of Fashion

*The world of fashion has evolved from 1900 to 2010 and continues to change today.*

## The Mood of the Collection

After a designer has done their research and picked some influences, they then create a mood board. Caroline Tatham and Julian Seaman wrote, "[Mood boards are] the first stage of organizing your thoughts and collected images, enabling you to channel your creative excitement toward a cohesive and targeted design outcome."[8] A designer creates a mood board by arranging their images and colors on a large board. Displaying their random thoughts and inspiration like this helps them decide if the images and colors they have chosen will work well together and if they need to eliminate or add more colors or influences. Fabric swatches and other materials are also useful additions to a mood board.

A clear mood board may help them create a successful collection. As they edit and narrow down influences and colors, key influences appear, and they have an easier time designing their collection. Designers also try to limit themselves to one mood board per collection so that their work will be focused and cohesive.

*Designers create mood boards to help them organize their thoughts regarding a future collection. They gather all their influences, inspirations, colors, textures, and other ideas all into one place.*

## Smart Clothing

Smart clothing is starting to become more popular as technology continues to develop. This type of clothing is created when designers combine sensor technology with clothing. Although most smart clothing is currently geared for athletes or gym enthusiasts, more companies are creating clothing that is fashionable and includes technology. Levi's was the first company to create a piece of clothing that connects to Google's Project Jacquard technology platform. This platform weaves touch and gestures into textiles. Wearers of Levi's jacket are able to utilize different Google services by pressing and swiping the jacket. Neviano, a French fashion technology company, created a line of swimsuits that warns the wearer when they have been in the sun too long. The sensor monitors the temperature and beeps to indicate when the wearer should apply more sunscreen. As technology improves, smart clothing will become an important part of fashion in the future.

### Illustrating a Collection

Fashion illustrations are the next step in the process and are meant to convey a designer's thoughts and ideas to the rest of the team. Typically, the illustrations are not completely realistic or drawn to scale. The illustrations exaggerate key elements or details that a designer is hoping to incorporate into the collection. Designers often go through several iterations of drawings for a design to get it right. Clothing for fashion illustrations can only be accurately drawn if the designer understands how the body lays within the clothing. Draping and folding of cloth is extremely important when designing clothes.

Fashion designers try to reflect their audience with their illustrations. If they are designing for menswear, their models will look different than the designs that another designer is creating for a womenswear collection. Additionally, how the illustration is done is important to the collection. Illustrations drawn with thin lines convey a different sense of the collection than illustrations drawn with thick, bold lines.

Finally, with the evolution of technology, more designers are using computer-aided design (CAD) programs to create their designs. Of course, hand-drawn illustrations are still important in the beginning stages of draft designs. Now, however, designers also have the option of using technology to portray their thoughts and then uploading them directly to other members of the design team or even to the textile designers. Then, edits can be made more quickly and effectively on the screen than if the designer was working with hand-drawn illustrations.

# Computer-Aided Design (CAD)

When someone thinks of fashion design, they may immediately think of hand-drawn designs first. However, with the development of technology and different CAD programs, more fashion designers are using computers. CAD is able to help with creating accurately sized designs, making design changes faster and easier, and experimenting with different designs. CAD gives designers the ability to change colors and draping precisely on computer models, which saves time on prototypes and other adjustments during the design process. The most popular CAD program is Adobe Illustrator, but there are other programs such as CorelDRAW, C-Design Fashion, and Optitex that are cheaper alternatives for fashion design students and young designers. Technology is always changing, so new CAD programs are coming out all the time, with enhancements and improvements to current technology. New fashion designers should ensure that they are comfortable working with CAD programs to increase their chances of success.

## Creating a Collection

Once the illustrations for the collection are final, the designers must still consider many more elements. The collection should have a cohesive motif, color scheme, fabric, and texture.

One of the most important things for a designer to remember is their audience. Depending on what type of collection they are designing, the audience will affect their collection differently. If they are a haute couture designer, they are creating tailored works of art for private clients. Their designs must meet the needs and desires of the audience exactly. A ready-to-wear designer has more leeway in what they design. Some of them, such as Japanese designer Junya Watanabe, often create designs that the average person would have trouble wearing. Their works are purely design based, playing with different cuts, fabrics, and finishing techniques. Watanabe is not motivated by how many designs he can sell, but by innovation within fashion design. Despite the fact that the average shopper would probably never buy his designs, his innovative designs still affect the entire fashion design world. A designer needs to be careful, however, as there is a thin line between truly innovating and over-exaggerating a design to hide a lack of skill or ideas. Mass-market designers must create clothing that the average person would find wearable, while still tapping into the fashion design trends of the haute couture and ready-to-wear collections. These designers must create designs that will create the most profit for the company.

*Some designers still create hand drawn representations of their designs. However, they may also use computer-aided design (CAD) programs.*

## Fashion Week 101

Typically, fall and spring are the two primary seasons when designers show their collections. However, depending on what type of fashion they are designing, they may present more collections throughout the year. Haute couture collections require extensive time and money to produce, so they generally will not have more than two showings a year. On the other hand, there tend to be multiple mass-market collections every year because they are cheaper and faster to produce. Customers expect new items in stores such as Target and Nordstrom all the time.

The fall collection is one of the usual showings for most fashion designers. Traditionally, fall colors are black, gray, and brown. Often these colors are accented with the 'it' color of the season. Typically, the fabrics used are heavier, in preparation for the colder weather. Of course, rules are always made to be broken. The spring collection is the other typical seasonal showing. There is generally a focus on layered clothing made out of cotton, knits, or other lighter fabrics. Colors for spring collections tend to be saturated and bold. Again, this is just the typical collection. There have been many successful designers who ignored these traditions.

There are also smaller capsule collections throughout the year, such as holiday or resort, which designers can use to break up the routine of the fall and spring collections. Holiday collections tend to be dressy and flashy, designed for special occasions during the festive winter months. Resort-themed collections tend to be bright or pastel to remind audiences of the tropics. Swimsuits and some spring clothes are often included in these collections.

Fashion week is an exciting, glamorous, and stress-filled event, in which the top fashion designers from all over the world exhibit their newest collections for everyone to see. It is the culmination of thousands of hours of design work and the crowning achievement of every fashion designer. Different fashion designers have made their fashion shows into displays of art and creativity. Jean Paul Gaultier's shows have included model Coco Rocha dancing an Irish jig down the runway one season and the runway serving as a Paris nightclub with silk maxi gowns and champagne another season. Alexander McQueen's fashion shows were also known for being outrageously over-the-top and once included a model standing in an actual ring of fire.

Fashion weeks occur twice a year, typically in February and September. The February shows highlight what upcoming items will be sold in stores in the fall and winter seasons, and the September collections show what will be in stores during the spring and summer seasons. Every year, four fashion weeks occur throughout the major cities in the world: New York City, London, Milan, and Paris. There are hundreds of other fashion weeks throughout the world, and sometimes these regional

*Fashion week runway shows are held all over the world. Shown here is a fashion show during Lamke Fashion Week in Mumbai, India.*

fashion weeks are good sources of new design talent.

Fashion weeks are extremely important since every showing can make or break a designer. Fashion buyers for large retailers such as Nordstrom and Macy's are invited to all the collections, and they make immediate decisions on whether or not they will order those designs for the upcoming seasons. Fashion editors not only forecast trends based on what designers show, but they also make critical decisions on which items they love and showcase them in their magazines. Finally, Hollywood stylists and stars attend and decide what pieces they might wear in the upcoming season. Their influence is critical as well, since what they are seen wearing is imitated by many people.

Although there is no official board that oversees which designers can show their collections, influence and seniority are crucial to getting one of the limited spots, especially during a specific time slot. Budget issues can also affect whether a designer can show his or her collection during a fashion week. An average show "costs about $150,000, though many are produced for less and certainly many for more."[9] Designers will typically show in the city where their studio is based. This makes it easier to handle any last minute changes, while also showing support for the local fashion industry.

A collection typically consists of 30 to 40 different pieces, which models wear as they strut down the runway. The show can run anywhere from 10 to 30 minutes, depending on how complicated the designer makes the show. The designs that are shown during a collection are typically more artistic in expression than what may show up in the store. They convey the general theme and idea of the designer's collection, but more commercial, modified versions of the runway designs will appear in stores. Runway shows are meant to evoke the ideas that inspired the designer, but what the models are wearing may not always be the most wearable item to the average person. Plus, a simple T-shirt and jeans ensemble on the runway will not impress critical fashion editors and buyers.

Fashion shows are not open to the public. Coveted front row seats for the best fashion shows are typically reserved for top-tier fashion editors, such as Anna Wintour, the current editor-in-chief of *Vogue* or Bridget Foley of *Women's Wear Daily*, actresses such as Jennifer Lawrence and Blake Lively, or popular bloggers such as Susie Lau of *Style Bubble*. The average person, thanks to modern technology, is able to view many runway shows that are live-streamed via different fashion blogs and magazines.

The first New York Fashion Week started in 1943, when Americans were not able to cross the Atlantic Ocean to see the fashion trends in Paris. The runways were consolidated in the Bryant Park area in 1994 for about 15 years. In 2010, they moved to Damrosch

Park outside of Lincoln Center. Most designers show their collections at this venue in the tents. However, more and more designers are going offsite to other venues, either to accommodate their fashion show needs, or because of budget issues.

Other global cities have also started their own fashion weeks. Sydney, Australia, and Mumbai, India, are two major cities that also host fashion weeks twice a year. Many of these cities showcase local talent and bring global attention to those designers. The local fashion weeks can jumpstart a young designer's career. These cities all aspire to be the fifth city included in the global fashion week lineup.

Creating one collection takes an unimaginable amount of time and effort. When creating multiple successful collections, a designer needs to constantly keep an open mind and always challenge themselves to create something better. Successful designers know that their message and product must always be consistent from season to season. Although the message and theme may evolve, it must always remain true to the brand to be consistently successful.

CHAPTER THREE

# Careers in Fashion Design

There is a vast difference between taking fashion design classes at school and entering the professional world of fashion design. Obtaining internships with different fashion design companies can be vital in helping a new graduate succeed, and there is a variety of careers in fashion design to choose from.

There are several important qualities that successful fashion designers have. Creativity and artistic ability are important since designers must create new and stylish designs, often with the same materials that their competitors are using. Designers must be able to convey their creative ideas through illustrations. The ability to make decisions is important, since designers are often working on deadlines and have exposure to many ideas and thoughts. Without being decisive, a designer would be overwhelmed from all the pressure and never make a decision on what fabric to use or what pieces to include in a collection. Finally, being detail-oriented is also important. Designers must have an eye to see what colors will make a design work. They must also pay attention to an entire design, ensuring that all the details work together, both functionally and aesthetically.

Most jobs related to fashion are found in big cities, such as New York or Paris. It is harder to find fashion jobs in smaller cities, so amateur designers should be willing to relocate to big cities. A career in this field often also requires traveling to many different countries to find inspiration for the next collection, attending trade or fashion shows, or visiting manufacturers to ensure quality control.

*Designers must be decisive and detail-oriented if they want to be successful in the field of fashion.*

## Jobs in the Fashion Industry

There are different types of designers within the fashion industry, including fashion, textile, and accessories. A fashion designer could be so bold as to create their own design house, such as Tommy Hilfiger or Vera Wang. Fashion designers can also aspire to be creative directors, who lead design teams within a luxury design house, such as Chanel or Versace. The final type of fashion designer is one who creates designs for retail stores. Within fashion, there are also different types of apparel that a designer can create, such as sportswear, special occasion, or outerwear. These clothing styles all require entirely different types of designs and deal with different types of fabrics. The United States Bureau of Labor Statistics has estimated that the median pay for fashion designers was $63,670 in May 2015, and the "employment of fashion designers is projected to grow by 3 percent from 2014 to 2024,"[10] meaning that there will be a lot of competition in this field in the future.

Textile designers work primarily with yarns and fabrics. Textile designers can work for fabric manufacturers, creating and designing the weaves and constructions of fabrics out of different materials. Some work inside a design house and produce the designs for a collection, while others work for a textile print house and sell those designs to a designer each season.

Accessories designers generally design products worn in addition to clothing, such as purses or shoes. These products can complement a fashion designer's collection or stand on their own. Costume design is suited to those who are interested in history and skilled with using different fabrics, forms, and colors to design for a particular film or drama.

Becoming a stylist is another option for designers. Instead of dealing with the time, stress, and energy of designing several collections a year, a stylist aids customers in choosing the perfect outfit. Stylists can also work with a designer in distributing a cohesive brand and story about the new collection. To be successful as a stylist, networking is more crucial than it is for the other fashion careers. A similar profession involves designing showrooms, fashion shows, or retail store windows.

Another option is to become a production manager. This role requires more of a process-oriented mind, not necessarily a creative one, but it is still important for ensuring that the products are of a certain quality and get to customers on time. Production managers work closely with designers to ensure that designs are created and manufactured according to a timeline. They also make sure these designs reach stores in time for the season to achieve maximum sales. With the increase of interest in environmental effects, there is a move toward "zero waste" production, where little material goes to waste.

Retail managers and buyers both need to focus on upcoming fashion trends. The store buyer must understand

*Social media platforms have become an important outlet for fashion designers to promote their products.*

the customers and their needs, as well as how those needs will be met by future trends. Some retail stores have buyers that purchase products for all the retail stores, and others have buyers who buy different products for each individual store. Successful store buyers have to be able to predict what items will fly off the shelves. The job outlook for buyers is only "projected to grow 2 percent from 2014 to 2024, [which is] slower than the average for all occupations."[11] The median wage for this job was $59,620 in May 2015. Retail managers should have a good grasp of how to display new products and inform their customers of upcoming trends.

Another career option is to be part of the fashion media, including columnists, photographers, and bloggers. A fashion columnist needs to understand fashion history and how it correlates to current trends. Designer collections need to be analyzed and critiqued, especially to see where trends are heading. Fashion bloggers have become increasingly visible and important at fashion weeks. Just like *Vogue* used to report on new trends that were displayed at horse races, fashion bloggers now report on their favorite style trends to millions of their followers through social media outlets such as blogs, Instagram, Snapchat, and Facebook.

A fashion public relations (PR) representative must research and understand the market to successfully represent a fashion house and ensure people are talking positively about the brand. The PR representative must also ensure that the reputation of the fashion house remains intact and positive throughout all events, especially when fashion collections are shown. The PR representative must have a charming and outgoing personality to genuinely represent their clients positively.

Another career in fashion design is the fashion illustrator. Traditionally, fashion illustrators worked at design houses and helped capture the thoughts and ideas of designers, or they created fashion illustrations for magazine covers. However, as photography grew in popularity, many fashion illustrators found themselves obsolete. With the recent spike in social media, the demand for fashion illustrators has once again increased. Many fashion illustrators post their drawings on Instagram and sell their artwork to their followers. This success can turn into additional jobs with design companies or advertising agencies. A strong design background and online presence are both crucial to succeed as a fashion illustrator.

## Get Involved!

There are several important organizations and associations within the fashion industry. Founded in 1962 by Eleanor Lambert, the Council of Fashion Designers of America (CFDA) is a not-for-profit association of designers in the United States. The CFDA has played an important part in promoting American fashion and putting it on the

*Shown here is the famous designer Diane von Furstenberg announcing the winner of the CFDA Fashion Icon Award at the 2016 CFDA Fashion Awards in New York City.*

## Get Schooled

Is it required to attend a fashion school to become a successful fashion designer? Not necessarily. There are some successful designers who have degrees in completely unrelated majors. However, that is not the norm. Fashion schools teach practical design skills, expose a student to how the fashion industry works, and give them access to successful alumni. Currently, many designers are utilizing technology and design software to illustrate their designs. Design schools will teach students how to use these tools. Almost every fashion school also helps their students to develop their portfolios, which can be crucial to getting a job after graduation. Fashion students also have the opportunity to enter different amateur fashion designer competitions, which helps them to develop their portfolios, along with getting them exposure to successful fashion designers. There are several lists of top fashion schools in the world, which generally include Central Saint Martins; London College of Fashion; and Parsons, the New School of Design.

global fashion industry map. Now, the CFDA boasts a membership of more than 500 fashion designers. In 1980, the first annual CFDA Fashion Awards were held. This awards ceremony recognizes and honors the top American fashion designers, along with emerging talent. The CFDA also hosts the CFDA/Vogue Fashion Fund to encourage young and emerging fashion talent by granting monetary prizes and business mentoring from other successful fashion designers.

Another important organization is the United States Fashion Industry Association (USFIA). It was founded in 1989, and its goal is to increase trade in the fashion industry on a global basis. The USFIA represents all members of the fashion industry, including retailers, importers, and apparel brands. It is headquartered in Washington, D.C., and keeps close ties with regulatory agencies to ensure that the fashion industry does not deal with regulatory barriers that it cannot overcome.

## Fashion Industry Outlook

The best way for someone to decide what career path to take in design is to get involved in anything related to fashion. They should work in retail stores to understand how they work and read as many fashion magazines and blogs as possible. They should also research who the important fashion designers are, what the new trends are, and create a strong fashion network by attending fashion industry events. Interning at different fashion companies to understand how different designers operate is useful. Finally, a fashion student should try to create their own path, whether through a blog or another social media channel.

The fashion industry is always changing and interconnected. There are many designers who started out in one role and then moved through numerous different careers to end up in their current job. It is important for a fashion student starting a career in design to create their own identity and do what they love.

CHAPTER FOUR

# Fashion Industry Issues

The fashion industry often seems glamorous and exciting, but like any other industry, it has its issues, too. It has been criticized for taking advantage of young girls and overemphasizing a thin frame as the perfect body shape. There are also issues of exploitation of workers in third world countries, which is fueled by the fast fashion industry in the Western world. Understanding the issues in fashion should influence the way people shop and design in the future. The industry needs to continue to work together and create ways to solve these problems.

## Pressure to Stay Thin

One issue that has been hotly debated for decades is the dangerously thin and underage models that parade down the runway every season. Kate Moss started the "heroin chic" look in the 1990s, in which models were extremely thin. This look then became the ideal image for designers and has affected not only the industry but also the health of many women around the world. It took until 2011 for the CFDA to release guidelines recommending the industry not use models that were under 16 years old or had evidence of eating disorders. The guidelines were not only to ensure that models were healthy, but also to address concerns that the fashion industry has a significant influence on young girls and boys. Several countries, including Israel, Italy, and Spain, have also passed legislation setting minimum weights and ages for female models.

There are many stories about how models maintain their thin figures, many of which are unhealthy. Some skip meals, and some are hovering on the brink of starvation. These young women are not healthy, and yet they are held up as the ideal image and size that many women aspire to be. Kirstie Clements, former editor of Australian *Vogue*, mentioned one instance where she had to work with a model who barely ate during a weeklong photo shoot. According to Clements, by the end of the week, "she didn't have the energy to even sit up; she could barely open her eyes. We actually had her lie down next to a fountain to get the last shot."[12] Models are more prone to dying at a young age from eating disorders, such as anorexia nervosa. Models Ana Carolina Reston, Luisel Ramos, and Isabelle Caro were all in their 20s when they died from anorexia-related issues.

There are many reasons designers give for why they prefer very thin models. Designers think their clothes fit and look better on thinner models, so the sample pieces that they design typically only fit on thin women. Clothes also tend to drape and flow more on tall, thin models, so this is what designers look for when they choose which models will wear their pieces. Models must fit into these scraps of fabric to work, and as models are paid per engagement, many go to extreme measures to be thin enough to fit into the samples that designers send. Designers also like to use younger girls because they have not gone through puberty yet, so designers do not have to work around natural curves. Finally, the smaller sample pieces also allow designers to create outfits with less fabric, which costs them less money. Essentially, models are made to fit into the clothes. Models are even often called "hangers."

"Thinspiration," a trend that glorifies being thin, has been around for a number of years. Social media accounts, such as Pinterest, Tumblr, and Instagram have all helped to spread this trend of idolizing thinness, especially in models. Many "thinspiration" images come from fashion show runways or fashion magazine ads. Although it is difficult to change the current ideal of beauty, some fashion designers have developed a sense of responsibility to protect women, especially young girls, and send the message that true ideal beauty is a healthy body, no matter what shape or size.

## The Struggle Is Real

Some people in the fashion industry also suffer from mental health issues, including depression and low self-esteem. A study done by the genetics company deCODE in the United Kingdom found that creative minds are 25 percent more likely to suffer from a mental health issue. Both designers and models are expected to be successful at all times, pushing themselves to impossibly high levels of perfection. Since most designers have multiple shows a year, all of which are highly publicized, there is tremendous pressure to be successful. Many designers work around the clock during fashion weeks, draining them emotionally, mentally, and physically. Success can result in millions of dollars from buyers and investors, and failure can destroy a designer's entire career. Having to deal with this pressure many times a year is very difficult and stressful.

One of the most recent tragedies is that of designer Alexander McQueen, who committed suicide in 2010. He struggled with depression for many years and had a history of drug abuse. He was severely affected by the suicide of his close friend and benefactor, Isabella Blow, in 2007, and the death of his mother a few days before he died. His death shocked the fashion design world and highlighted the fact that mental health is a huge issue in the fashion world, affecting even a prolific and successful fashion designer such as McQueen.

Models also deal with a lot of pressure, and studies that compare models with other occupations show that their "mental health is poorer and life satisfaction is lower. Despite their earning power and status as icons of beauty, the models rated lower on measures of happiness, psychological fulfillment and feelings of competence."[13] Many models deal with lives of constant travel and a job where they are viewed as commodities, valued based on just their looks. This life also leaves them with little time to develop close friendships or relationships, especially since many of them start modeling at young ages, when they are still beginning to develop physically and emotionally. During their travels, young models typically do not have any guardians to take care of them, either physically or emotionally. The only thing that they can control is their body, so many of them struggle with depression, anorexia, and other disorders. Constant criticism of their body from modeling agencies, designers, or their peers all contributes to these issues. Young models also struggle with being exploited by others in the industry, being directed to just do what they are told, regardless of whether or not they feel comfortable with it; otherwise, they are told they will not get another job. Young models do not know how to say "no" yet, and this also has a detrimental effect on their mental health.

The fashion industry is beginning to discuss how to deal with mental health issues, but there is still much work to be done. The mental health of both models and designers needs to be a major focus for all in this industry to allow this entire artistic community to thrive without suffering any more losses of great talents.

*Shown here is the late designer Alexander McQueen at one of the last fashion shows he presented before his death in 2010. McQueen's death helped shed a light on mental health issues within the world of fashion design.*

## Fashion Rivalries

It is also no secret that the fashion industry is notoriously competitive. Often, these rivalries spill out into the public eye. One of the most famous rivalries was between Coco Chanel and Elsa Schiaparelli. Both women were self-made fashion designers, with no formal training, fighting for the public's love. During the 1920s and 1930s, Schiaparelli's designs were seen as bolder and more innovative than Chanel's. Although Chanel was also innovative, her designs were more elegant and classic. Schiaparelli's designs were daring, especially her famous lobster dress. Schiaparelli and Chanel often publicly made comments about each other. Schiaparelli called Chanel "that milliner," and Chanel dismissed Schiaparelli as "that Italian artist who makes clothes."[14] Chanel even once set Schiaparelli on fire during a costume party. During World War II, Chanel closed her shop. Schiaparelli, however, stayed in France, and continued to travel between New York City and Paris, despite the German occupation of France. Rumors spread about both of their involvement with the Nazis. After the war, women in society began to gravitate towards the "New Look" of Christian Dior. Finally, in 1954, after feeling the economic effects of the war, Schiaparelli shut her house down for good, whereas Chanel successfully came back that year from her retirement. Chanel's label is still popular today.

Another epic rivalry that has spanned decades was between Yves Saint Laurent and Karl Lagerfeld. Both men had similar upbringings and even studied together at a school in Paris. Some speculate that their rivalry began in 1954, when both won prizes in the International Wool Secretariat fashion design competition. After graduation, Yves Saint Laurent began his rise to success at the haute couture company of Christian Dior. Lagerfeld, on the other hand, called haute couture a dying art, and began freelance designing ready-to-wear clothes. Similar to the style difference between Schiaparelli and Chanel, Yves Saint Laurent focused on female elegance, whereas Lagerfeld's designs were eclectic and outrageous. Outside of fashion designing, in the early 1970s, Yves Saint Laurent had an affair with Lagerfeld's then-boyfriend, Jacques de Bascher, and essentially stole him from Lagerfeld. This affair only increased the animosity between the designers. After multiple public barbs, this rivalry finally faded in 2002, when Yves Saint Laurent retired from the fashion scene, and it stopped altogether with his death in 2008. Today, Lagerfeld is still an icon in the fashion industry, maintaining his success at Chanel and other labels.

## "Fast Fashion"

Another big issue in the fashion industry today is "fast fashion." Zara introduced this concept by beginning to restock new designs in its stores twice a week, instead of once a season. Now, fashion cycles are moving faster than ever, with customers demanding trends in stores as soon as they are seen on the runway. Brands such as Forever 21, Uniqlo, Zara, and H&M are mass-producing these trends at an extremely fast rate for low prices. They are even restocking their stores on a daily basis. Their affordable prices attract more customers and increase profits for these companies, and these successful retailers have grown at a rate of almost 10 percent over the past five years. However, this success comes with a price, as there are many ethical issues that come with cheap clothing, especially sustainability and human rights.

A customer is more likely to dispose of the clothes that they buy at cheaper prices, and "according to the Environmental Protection Agency, 15.1 million tons of textile waste was generated in 2013, of which 12.8 million tons were discarded."[15] That is a disposal rate of almost 85 percent. Although some of this discarded clothing can be exported to other countries, such as India, Russia, and Pakistan, most of it is made so poorly that it must be discarded. This creates a huge amount of textile waste, which hurts the environment, as many of the materials take years to decompose in landfills, and the chemicals on the clothes can leach into the groundwater.

In addition, a lot of environmental pollution occurs during the life cycle of a piece of clothing: Pesticides and large amounts of water are used for cotton production, toxic dyes are used in manufacturing, pollutants are produced by ships transporting clothes from Asia to North America and Europe, and landfills are filled with non-biodegradable textiles. Out of all the clothing worn in the United States today, only 2 percent is actually made in America. It takes 1,849 gallons (7,000 L) of water to produce a typical pair of jeans, and it takes more than 713 gallons (2,700 L) of water to make a single T-shirt. That amount of water is how much a person would typically drink over the course of 900 days, or almost 3 years. Then, 1.8 million tons (1.7 million mt) of chemicals are used throughout the dyeing process. The fashion industry emits more than 937 tons (850,032 mt) of carbon dioxide each year.

Some clothing retailers are attempting to decrease their impact on the environment by creating clothing recycle programs or introducing garments made out of recycled textiles. However, "only [0].1 percent of all clothing collected by charities and take-back programs is recycled into textile fiber."[16]

Other concepts have sprung up, such as renting clothes instead of owning them. The company Rent the Runway allows the customer to rent designer clothes and then return them. There are other companies who are starting to rent clothes out as well. On an individual basis, a customer can begin to invest in higher quality clothes, instead of buying the cheapest clothes. There are many companies now who proudly display the way they create clothes sustainably. Although their clothes are more expensive than those of fast fashion stores, they are of higher quality.

Finally, there are reports of child labor in cotton fields in countries such as China, India, and other third world nations that mainly produce cotton for fast fashion companies. In addition, many of the workers who are of legal age are paid pennies each day.

A Free2Work 2012 report found that of companies investigated "only 2% were able to pay a wage … to cover basic living requirements."[17] If demand for fast fashion, which includes $1.80 camisoles and $7.80 jeans, continues to climb at its current rate, clothing retailers will have little incentive to change their current processes.

There have been some attempts to address the issues of sustainability and human rights. Several countries have created agreements to better working conditions for factory and cotton

This large amount of textile waste was thrown away at a sewing factory's disposal dump site. Fashion may be an art, but it creates a lot of ugly pollution.

workers, such as the Bangladesh Accord on Fire and Building Safety and the Uzbek Cotton Pledge. The Greenpeace Detox Campaign is another attempt by an organization to regulate the amount of hazardous chemicals and dyes that are used during the manufacturing process. Some companies, such as Uniqlo and H&M, have adopted these solutions, but others, such as Forever 21, have not adopted a single one.

## Fakes Are Never in Fashion

Counterfeits cost the fashion industry billions of dollars each year. In 2013, the World Trademark Review

estimated that counterfeit goods generate “between $500 to $600 billion annually.”[18]

During the 1990s, fake handbags were popular because of the logomania that swept society. Handbags were easily recognizable as luxury items and status symbols, especially with their flashy logos. Everyone wanted a handbag, and few people thought about the reasons why a luxury handbag was only $50 instead of $500.

*Counterfeit purses, such as the ones shown here, are popular items around the world because they provide people with an inexpensive status symbol.*

# Unsafe Working Conditions

The deadliest disaster in the fashion industry occurred on April 24, 2013, when the Rana Plaza clothing factory collapsed in Bangladesh. This tragedy killed more than 1,000 people and revealed how horrible factory conditions can be. Bangladesh is the world's second-largest exporter of ready-to-wear clothes, just behind China. In Bangladesh, the minimum monthly wage for a clothing factory worker is just $68, and many factory owners exploit their workers. This event forced many companies to look into working conditions in their overseas factories. The Bangladeshi factory was constructed with substandard materials, with no regard to building codes. Many workers were forced to work 14-hour days, with no breaks or drinking water to cool off in the intense heat. The owners of the Rana Plaza have been charged with murder, since they were warned about the unsafe working conditions but still forced the workers to continue. However, there are still many factories that exist with horrible working conditions, not only abroad, but also in Western countries. Fashion companies need to ensure that factories obey new laws about proper working conditions.

*This photograph of the Rana Plaza clothing factory in Bangladesh was taken the day after the deadly building collapse.*

Many people either do not realize or ignore the fact that counterfeit goods support child labor and sweatshop conditions. These goods have even been linked to terrorist organizations. Different government enforcement agencies have attempted to stop counterfeit fashion activity, but with the increase of e-commerce, it has become increasingly difficult to track each instance of counterfeit sale. Europe has laws against purchasing counterfeit products, but the United States does not.

Plagiarism is also an issue. There is little intellectual property protection for fashion like there is for other creative works, such as art or literature. Although this is an issue with cheap counterfeits, it has become an ever-present issue with fast fashion companies. Since fast fashion is typically based on a three-week cycle time, it is able to produce cheaper and lower quality versions of what is seen on a runway. Instead of paying hundreds of dollars for a dress from Anna Sui or Jason Wu, a customer will pay $30 for a similar dress from Forever 21 that they can purchase and wear immediately.

The counterfeit fashion industry has become extremely good at producing fakes. Customers may not even realize that they have purchased a fake, as online marketing tactics often trick them into paying full price for a fake product online. In addition, the market has grown to a point where many shoppers are deal seekers, always searching for the best prices on fashion items online. Counterfeiters are able to target these customers with websites that may look similar to legitimate luxury brand sites but redirect customers to purchase fake items.

## Every Body Is Beautiful

The Fashion Spot's Runway Diversity Report Spring 2017 "examined 299 shows and 8,832 model appearances in New York City, London, Paris and Milan. For the first time in recent history, more than 25 percent of the model castings were nonwhite."[19] These statistics have been increasing slightly every season. In the fall 2016 report, 24.7 percent of models were people of color, and the spring 2016 report showed that 22.4 percent of models were people of color. New York City had the highest diversity rating in the spring 2017 report, with 30.3 percent of its models representing people of color, but this was less than the previous season, when 31.9 percent of its models were people of color. In 2014, 44 of the biggest fashion magazines published 611 covers, and only 19 percent of those covers featured non-white models. In addition, 90 percent of the models in fashion advertising campaigns were white.

The gap between diversity in the fashion industry and the actual customer base is increasingly becoming a problem in the luxury market. The diversity of people who are buying luxury fashion has increased tremendously, with Asia and Africa's shares of the luxury market growing exponentially in the past few years. However, few models who walk the fashion week runways are from those areas. The industry needs to work to bridge this gap between diversity in the fashion industry and diversity in their customers. Within mass-market fashion, models in advertisements and marketing tend to be more ethnically diverse, since these companies are catering to their customers.

This diversity issue is mirrored in designers as well as models. Out of the 470 designers who are part of the CFDA, only 12 are African American, and this number has decreased over the years. In the 1970s, the percentage of black designers was higher than it is today, so designers such as Willi Smith, Stephen Burrows, and Scott Barrie had much more of an impact than black designers have today. Although the percentage of Asians in the CFDA is higher than the percentage of African Americans, the low numbers of minority designers overall still impact a minority designer's progress in the fashion industry. Across the fashion industry—fashion editors, fashion buyers, and those who wear the latest fashions—white women still mainly hold these positions. Often, designers are inspired by trends in diverse cultures, yet this diversity is not reflected in who is chosen to represent it.

Age is another issue in the fashion industry; there were only 13 models aged 50 and above on the women's runways in recent years. The average age of the female model is 22, but the average age of women who typically buy luxury fashion is over 35.

There are several fashion industry supporters who are vocal about increasing the diversity in the fashion industry, especially Bethann Hardison and Naomi Campbell. A 30-year fashion industry veteran, Campbell has been a leader in fashion diversity as the first black model on the cover of *Vogue Paris* and also the first black model on the cover of *Vogue*'s legendary September issue. She continually encourages designers to cast models of all ethnicities. A former model, Hardison is the founder of the Diversity Coalition, which works to promote racial diversity in the industry. In 2014, Hardison won the CFDA Founder's Award for her work. She is constantly thinking of different ways to encourage designers to include diverse models in their shows, including creating guidelines for racial diversity, writing to designers who have whitewashed model lineups, and highlighting diverse models through photos and interviews online.

There is no defined percentage to indicate when the fashion industry will have become diverse "enough," but there is still definite room for progress within the fashion industry. Art often reflects society, and many are calling for the fashion industry to be a more accurate reflection of global diversity. Advocates will continue to bring up this issue until all races and ethnicities are represented within the modeling world.

Some fashion show runways are becoming more inclusive places that reflect different races and beauty standards, as this Leanne Marshall runway from 2016 shows.

## Awareness in the Industry

These are all issues that the fashion industry deals with. As the industry continues to grow and evolve, some of the issues will be resolved, and others will arise. Designers should be aware of these issues as they continue to work within the industry and look for ways to resolve them if possible. Many of these issues can only be solved with the support of everyone in the industry.

# What's Next? The Future of Fashion

Fashion has been hugely influenced by the rise of the Internet and other advancements in technology. Technology has completely changed the way that people design and buy clothes, as well as what fashion trends are followed. Instead of only following direction from Paris fashion shows, people are able to decide what trends they would like to follow based on global street fashion or social media influencers.

## Hello World!

In 1994, with the advent of the Internet, e-commerce was born, and people began a whole new way of shopping. Consumers no longer need to go into physical brick-and-mortar shops but are able to look at all styles of fashion and design from the comfort of their home. A person can follow hundreds of different fashion blogs online and decide how they want to wear a certain trend based on their own style and shape. The Internet has also allowed for the creation of Internet-only retailers, such as Asos and Net-A-Porter, that do not have to pay for expensive brick-and-mortar storefronts. In addition, the ease of feedback, both in the form of online reviews and sales, has allowed for increased interaction between designers and consumers. People are also now able to resell clothes online through sites and apps such as eBay or Poshmark, which has become a popular way to find vintage designer items.

Michelle Obama has influenced fashion in a major way.

Fashion blogs have also allowed individuals to showcase their own styles, and many of them affect whether society follows certain trends. The most popular fashion blogs form partnerships or associations with fashion companies, allowing them to put their own spin on how to wear the newest and hottest items as they come out. This also affects sales and how people wear new trends.

Celebrities, especially music and movie stars, also influence trends. Hundreds of thousands of people followed Princess Diana's style, and people are now influenced by her son William's wife, Catherine, the Duchess of Cambridge, as well as other international figures such as former First Lady Michelle Obama. Often, the dresses and outfits that they wear are quickly sold out online, regardless if the item is from Zara, Target, or a high fashion label, such as Reiss or Jason Wu.

In addition, women are now openly mixing high fashion items, such as an expensive Coach purse, with fast fashion, such as a dress from H&M. Luxury brands are openly looking for collaborations with retail stores, and these collaborations are generally successful. In the past, women who were purchasing luxury brands were not interested in purchasing from retail or department stores and mixing the two types of clothing. Now, women want a diverse closet, which gives them the option to wear something that is trendier from a fast fashion retailer. However, they also want to buy investment pieces of clothing that they will be able to wear for many years, such as a classic trench coat or a white button down shirt. Consumers are following the lead of celebrities and other public figures, who are mixing high fashion and retail looks. With the increase in individuality, consumers are wearing whatever they want, no longer wearing the same brand from head to toe. Buying clothes from both luxury brands and fast fashion companies also creates many more fashion options that the customer can mix and style.

Individuals also now have easy access to many different styles, not only globally, but also throughout the decades. There is no single look that dictates what individuals wear each season, nor do individuals feel the need to conform to a single style for the season. Naturally, there are still some trends that are popular each season, but each person can make their own decisions, including what trends they follow, if any.

## Fresh Off the Streets

Street fashion has grown significantly since the late 1990s, and this term refers to fashion trends that are driven by people instead of by fashion designers. Street fashion trickles upward, with these trends first seen on the streets, then on designer runways. There have been several influential street fashion photographers since the development of the camera.

Eugène Atget was one of the first documenters of candid street life in Paris during the 1890s. Many people consider Henri Cartier-Bresson as one of the best street photographers ever as a result of his ability to capture simple photographs in natural light. In 1978, the *New York Times* launched its "On the Street" column, which showcased well-dressed women, shot by Bill Cunningham. Cunningham realized there was something missing: "I realized that you didn't know anything unless you photographed the shows and the street, to see how people interpreted what designers hoped they would buy. I realized that the street was the missing ingredient."[20] Instead of focusing on who he was shooting, or what brands they were wearing, Cunningham focused on elements that he liked in the clothes, such as the cut of a jacket. Sometimes, he ended up shooting celebrities, but only if they were wearing something interesting. Street style became popular because these faces of fashion were more relatable to customers than fashion models.

Starting in 2009, with Dolce & Gabbana, fashion shows began to invite popular street photographers to sit in the front rows of fashion shows. Now, photographers such as Scott Schuman of *The Sartorialist* and Yvan Rodic of *FaceHunter* have their own popular street style sites

## Japanese Street Fashion

Japan has long been one of the more progressive countries in terms of fashion trends. Many designers look to Tokyo when they are seeking inspirations for their collections. Japanese street fashion exploded in the 1990s as a way to rebel against the stagnation of the 1980s economic recession. Teenagers, especially, began to exhibit their individuality and creativity. Different shopping districts in Tokyo have their own fashion identities, including Harajuku, Ginza, and Shibuya. One style that Japanese youth wear, which is also popular in other countries, is cosplay, short for "costume play," where they dress up and act like popular fictional characters, typically from anime or manga. Another popular style is Lolita, where girls wear costumes inspired by the Victorian and Edwardian fashion eras. Shoichi Aoki, who is the founder of Tokyo's *Street*, *FRUiTS*, and *Tune* fashion magazines, began to document street style during this time. Fashion magazines still play a vital part in affecting the style of young Japanese girls, but they are decreasing in popularity, with the Internet increasing in importance. New fashion styles are constantly popping up in Japan and will continue to influence fashion worldwide.

*Shown here are young Japanese girls dressed in the Lolita style, which features modest clothing influenced by past historical eras.*

that capture street style globally. The streets outside of fashion weeks are now overrun by bloggers and fashion students who may not even be attending any of the shows but who want their outfits to get captured by the gauntlets of fashion street photographers who crowd the shows. There is as much buzz around what people are wearing outside the tents as there is around the models within the tents. Popular fashion bloggers, such as Gary Pepper Girl or The Glamourai, who post their own styled outfits, have showcased how trends can be interpreted on the streets by different fashion enthusiasts.

In 2013, Suzy Menkes, the international *Vogue* editor, wrote a piece for the *New York Times Style Magazine*, where she scornfully called the phenomenon of street fashion and photographers, "the circus of fashion."[21] Photographers now cram the steps to the fashion shows, snapping pictures of anyone they recognize, with little regard to who they may be running over. Companies are capitalizing on popular fashion bloggers by offering them pieces to wear from their new collections. As this avenue becomes more and more commercialized, Menkes and others are of the opinion that people will start to look for new ways to find fashion inspiration, somewhere where people are just dressing for themselves, not in what clothes designers send them. So far, social media apps such as Instagram and Snapchat have helped to continue street style's popularity.

## Social Media and Fashion

Social media has completely transformed the way the fashion industry operates. Instead of who a person knows in the industry or what positions they may have held, companies now consider the number of followers a person has on a certain social media account when picking who they want to cover their new collections. Brooklyn Beckham, the son of David and Victoria Beckham, was selected by Burberry to photograph a fragrance ad campaign in February 2016. Although there were plenty of people who criticized this decision, Burberry commented that, "Brooklyn has a really great eye for image and Instagram works brilliantly for him as a platform to showcase his work."[22] McKinsey, one of the top management consulting firms, found that 75 percent of all luxury purchases are influenced by what customers see and hear online. Fashion companies are recognizing the power and influence that leaders of social media can have on their brands, and the smart ones are capitalizing on this to bring more profit to their businesses.

Many companies are also utilizing social media to communicate directly with their customers. This connection allows designers to engage their customers in honest and authentic dialogue, which enhances the customer experience and increases the likelihood that the customer will purchase their products. People also leave reviews of products and companies on social media sites, which now impact how customers view a certain company. Companies can suffer significantly if negative reviews of their products are left online and there is no response from the company.

Companies are also using social media to predict upcoming trends in the fashion industry. Now more than ever, it is apparent that customers are creating the trends instead of following them. In addition, with the advent of technology, trends are coming and going even faster. For instance, in 2010, Twitter feedback from customers who wanted plus sizes from the brand Marc Jacobs impacted the CEO so much that he tweeted that he would start to design them. There has been a direct correlation between an increase in interaction with customers and sales. The new generation of customers are used to interacting online with the brands that they love and being able to see their feedback have an immediate impact. Many brands have made changes to sizing, designs, and colors based on customer feedback. However, fashion designers remain aware that they also need to keep their brand identity clear and consistent. There will always be customers who do not agree with what a designer has created. Designers need to take customer feedback into consideration when creating new designs but not necessarily create entire designs around what customers want.

## The Next Big Thing

With fashion trends being decided more often by people now instead of designers, it can be hard for a young designer to determine what to include in their collection. However, this has not stopped popular trendsetters such as *Vogue*, *Elle*, or other fashion magazines from declaring what they think are the new trends for the season. Since 2000, the company Pantone has also selected a Color of the Year that affects what colors are used in designs and eventually purchased by buyers. This color is chosen by color experts who carefully research what trends and influences are affecting buyers throughout the world. Oftentimes, this color is seen prominently on the fashion runways.

Fashion trends today are often influenced by what consumers are looking for. The current trend of athleisure was started completely by people who were looking to wear casual workout gear throughout the entire day. It has now become acceptable to wear items such as yoga pants throughout the day and even to business events. The United States is enjoying an increase in fitness-conscious customers who want to get fit while also looking fabulous. In addition, the athlesisure trend appeals to people who want to wear comfortable clothing, even if they are not working out. Athleisure has become part of a lifestyle of wellness. People ranging from celebrities, to CEOs, to the average person, have been seen wearing athleisure in recent years.

The brand lululemon has been successful with its line of yoga pants and has had tremendous growth for years, all of it due to the growing athleisure trend.

# The Sartorialist

Street photography has had an increasing impact on the fashion industry. Instead of fashion magazine editors making decisions about fashion, now anyone on the street can have a say as bloggers' outfits can reach as many viewers as, or even more than, a print fashion magazine. One of the most famous street photographers is Scott Schuman, who runs the popular blog *The Sartorialist*. Schuman began his blog in 2005 with the goal of "creating a two-way dialogue about the world of fashion and its relationship to daily life."[1] In 2009, Schuman was tapped by Burberry to help create a successful social media campaign called "Art of the Trench." He also ran his own column in *GQ* magazine for more than 3 years, while his blog receives more than 14 million monthly page views. On a regular basis, Schuman has the privilege of traveling to profile fashion in many different locations, including Paris, London, Milan, India, and Morocco. He does not focus on what someone is wearing or how much it costs, but on the details of each subject, such as their pose or the way their outfit works together. Appearing on *The Sartorialist* is seen as the ultimate honor for many, especially during fashion week.

1. "Biography," *The Sartorialist*. www.thesartorialist.com/biography/.

*Shown here is a model posing for street photographers during Milan Fashion Week in Italy in 2015.*

Athletic clothing brands such as Nike, Adidas, and Under Armour, as well as other clothing brands, such as Tory Burch, which is not focused on sports apparel, have increased their investments in athleisure clothing. It has been estimated by those with industry expertise that this trend will only increase in coming years.

As the world expands globally, trends are influenced by the arrival of new designers from all over the world, especially from Japan and Africa. Many designers travel to exotic destinations to get inspiration from the designs of Moroccan tile or Thailand's palaces. Fashion designers also began to reinvent looks from previous decades. Creative looks are now not only inspired by designs from the runway, but also from styles on the street. Clothing is more utilitarian, especially with unisex outfits of hooded sweatshirts, cargo pants, and parkas as the roles of women and men become more blurred in society. No one can accurately predict what the next trend will be, but designers can use different resources to develop their own inspirations and designs as they continue to grow as artists.

# NOTES

## Introduction: The Evolution of Fashion

1. Zhai Yun Tan, "What Happens When Fashion Becomes Fast, Disposable and Cheap?," NPR Environment, April 20, 2016. www.npr.org/2016/04/08/473513620/what-happens-when-fashion-becomes-fast-disposable-and-cheap.
2. Francesca Sterlacci and Joanne Arbuckle, *Historical Dictionary of the Fashion Industry*. Lanham, MD: The Scarecrow Press, Inc., 2008, p. xvi.

## Chapter One: History of Fashion Design

3. Valerie Mendes and Amy de la Haye, *20th Century Fashion*. New York, NY: Thames & Hudson, 1999, p. 36.
4. Karen Karbo, *The Gospel According to Coco Chanel: Life Lessons from the World's Most Elegant Woman*. Guilford, CT: skirt!, 2009.
5. Jacki Lyden, "Schiaparelli: The Shocking, Shadowed Life of a Fashion Icon," NPR Books, October 11, 2014. www.npr.org/2014/10/11/354636723/schiaparelli-the-shocking-shadowed-life-of-a-fashion-icon.
6. Simone Werle, *50 Famous Designers You Should Know*. New York, NY: Prestel Publishing, 2010, p. 87.
7. Valerie Mendes and Amy de la Haye, *Fashion Since 1900*. New York, NY: Thames & Hudson, 2010, p. 222.

## Chapter Two: Fashion Is Art

8. Caroline Tatham and Julian Seaman, *Fashion Design Drawing Course*. New York, NY: Quarto, Inc., 2003, p. 26.

9. Josh Patner, "Fashion Week FAQ," *Slate*, September 13, 2004. www.slate.com/articles/arts/fashion/2004/09/fashion_week_faq.html.

## Chapter Three: Careers in Fashion Design

10. Bureau of Labor Statistics, "Fashion Designers," *Occupational Outlook Handbook*, December 17, 2015. www.bls.gov/ooh/arts-and-design/fashion-designers.htm.
11. Bureau of Labor Statistics, "Buyers and Purchasing Agents," *Occupational Outlook Handbook*, December 17, 2015. www.bls.gov/ooh/business-and-financial/buyers-and-purchasing-agents.htm.

## Chapter Four: Fashion Industry Issues

12. Kirstie Clements, "Former Vogue Editor: The Truth About Size Zero," *The Guardian*, July 5, 2013. www.theguardian.com/fashion/2013/jul/05/vogue-truth-size-zero-kirstie-clements.
13. Jeremy Laurance, "Models' Mental Well-being Worse Than Their Peers," *Independent*, February 11, 2007. www.independent.co.uk/life-style/health-and-families/health-news/models-mental-well-being-worse-than-their-peers-436057.html.
14. "1930 Coco's Great Fashion Rivalry," Little Black Dress, www.littleblackdress.co.uk/life-of-chanel/cocos-great-fashion-rivalry.html.
15. Zhai Yun Tan, "What Happens When Fashion Becomes Fast, Disposable and Cheap?."
16. Alden Wicker, "Fast Fashion is Creating an Environmental Crisis," *Newsweek*, September 1, 2016. www.newsweek.com/2016/09/09/old-clothes-fashion-waste-crisis-494824.html.
17. Alden Wicker, "Fast Fashion—Can It Be Ethical?" *Good on You*, May 25, 2015. goodonyou.org.au/fast-fashion-can-it-be-ethical/.
18. Roxanne Elings, Lisa D. Keith, and George P. Wukoson, "Anti-counterfeiting in the Fashion and Luxury Sectors: Trends and Strategies," *World Trademark Review*, 2013. www.worldtrademarkreview.com/Intelligence/Anti-Counterfeiting/2013/Industry-insight/Anti-counterfeiting-in-the-fashion-and-luxury-sectors-trends-and-strategies.
19. Cordelia Tai, "Report: The Spring 2017 Runways Were the Most Diverse in History – Sort Of," *The Fashion Spot*, October 14, 2016. www.thefashionspot.com/runway-news/717823-diversity-report-spring-2017-runways/.

## Chapter Five: What's Next? The Future of Fashion

20. Bill Cunningham, "Bill Cunningham on Bill Cunningham," *New York Times*, June 25, 2016. www.nytimes.com/2016/06/26/fashion/bill-cunningham-on-his-life.html.
21. Nicole Phelps, "A Brief Oral History of Modern Street Style," *Vogue*, April 13, 2016. www.vogue.com/13425545/oral-history-modern-street-style/.
22. Katie Hope, "How Social Media is Transforming the Fashion Industry," *BBC News*, February 5, 2016. www.bbc.com/news/business-35483480.

# For More Information

## Books

Faerm, Steven. *Fashion Design Course*. New York, NY: Quarto, Inc., 2010.
This book has step-by-step exercises and tutorials on how to create fashion designs and includes advice on how to prepare for a fashion career.

McKelvey, Kathryn, and Janine Munslow. *Illustrating Fashion—2nd Edition*. Oxford, UK: Blackwell Publishing, 2007.
This book provides an overview on illustrating fashion designs both by hand and through the use of computer programs.

Sterlacci, Francesca, and Joanne Arbuckle. *Historical Dictionary of the Fashion Industry*. Lanham, MD: Scarecrow Press, 2008.
This book is a comprehensive guide on the history of fashion and terms used in the fashion industry.

Werle, Simone. *50 Fashion Designers You Should Know*. New York, NY: Prestel Publishing, 1997.
This book has short biographies on 50 influential fashion designers.

## Film

*The True Cost*, directed by Andrew Morgan (2015; Life is my Movie Entertainment), DVD.
This documentary is about the impact of the fashion industry. It covers the clothes, the people who make them, and their impact on the environment.

## Websites

**The Fashion Spot**
*www.thefashionspot.com/*

The Fashion Spot is a respected fashion industry website that includes a fashion community forum and relevant industry-focused articles, known especially for its biannual Diversity Reports.

**Fashionista: "The 25 Best Fashion Schools in the World in 2016"**
*fashionista.com/2016/06/best-fashion-colleges-2016*

This article includes Fashionista's annual list of the top fashion schools in the world.

**Occupational Outlook Handbook: "Fashion Designers"**
*www.bls.gov/ooh/arts-and-design/fashion-designers.htm*

This website has an overview of the fashion design profession, with outlook and training information.

***The Sartorialist***
*www.thesartorialist.com/*

This is one of the first street photographer fashion blogs, run by Scott Schuman.

***Vogue***
*www.vogue.com/*

This website is the online presence of one of the most popular and influential fashion magazines in the world.

# Index

## W



## Y



## Z

# Picture Credits

Cover Paolo Bona/Shutterstock.com; back cover vector illustration/Shutterstock.com; pp. 1, 3–4, 6, 15, 40, 58, 66, 83, 93, 96, 98, 103–104 (title paint splash) Lunarus/Shutterstock.com; p. 7 Pascal Le Segretain/Getty Images; pp. 9, 13, 17, 19, 23, 25, 28, 37, 43, 47, 49, 52, 54, 62, 69, 73, 77, 81, 87, 90 (caption paint splash) Jaroslav Machacek/Shutterstock.com; p. 9 FashionStock.com/Shutterstock.com; pp. 12–13 Imagno/Getty Images; p. 16 Brooklyn Museum Costume Collection at The Metropolitan Museum of Art, Gift of the Brooklyn Museum, 2009; Designated Purchase Fund, 1987; p. 17 Brooklyn Museum Costume Collection at The Metropolitan Museum of Art, Gift of the Brooklyn Museum, 2009; Gift of Edith Gardiner, 1926; p. 19 Edward Steichen/Condé Nast via Getty Images; p. 21 Silver Screen Collection/Getty Images; p. 22 Woman's Dress, 1937 (silk organza & horsehair), Italian School, (20th century) / Philadelphia Museum of Art, Pennsylvania, PA, USA / Gift of Mme Elsa Schiaparelli, 1969 / Bridgeman Images; p. 23 Keystone-France/Gamma-Keystone via Getty Images; pp. 24–25 Chicago History Museum/Getty Images; p. 26 Keystone/Getty Images; pp. 28–29 Giancarlo BOTTI/Gamma-Rapho via Getty Images; pp. 30–31 RDA/Getty Images; p. 32 Arthur Elgort/Condé Nast via Getty Images; p. 34 Vital9s/Shutterstock.com; p. 37 s_bukley/Shutterstock.com; p. 38 Scott Barbour/Getty Images; pp. 42–43 alionabirukova/Shutterstock.com; p. 44 GABRIEL BOUYS/AFP/Getty Images; pp. 46–47 sch/Shutterstock.com; pp. 48–49 Jon Feingersh/The Image Bank/Getty Images; pp. 52–53 vfedorchenko/Shutterstock.com; pp. 54–55 STRDEL/AFP/Getty Images; p. 59 g-stockstudio/iStock/Thinkstock; p. 61 happydancing/Shutterstock.com; pp. 62–63 Theo Wargo/Getty Images; p. 69 FRANCOIS GUILLOT/AFP/Getty Images; pp. 72–73 Gigira/Shutterstock.com; pp. 74–75 Ian Law/Shutterstock.com; pp. 76–77 MUNIR UZ ZAMAN/AFP/Getty Images; pp. 80–81 Sam Aronov/Shutterstock.com; p. 84 Everett Collection/Shutterstock.com; pp. 86–87 TOSHIFUMI KITAMURA/AFP/Getty Images; pp. 90–91 Eugenio Marongiu/Shutterstock.com.

# About the Author

**Ruth Huoh** has been obsessed with fashion design ever since she was born. Somehow, she ended up with a degree in Finance, and she spends all her money on shoes. When she has spare time, she loves traveling, doing crosswords, and redecorating her house. This is her first book for young adults.